2. *Weep, O mine eyes*

John Bennet (*c.*1575–after 1614)

BOB CHILCOTT

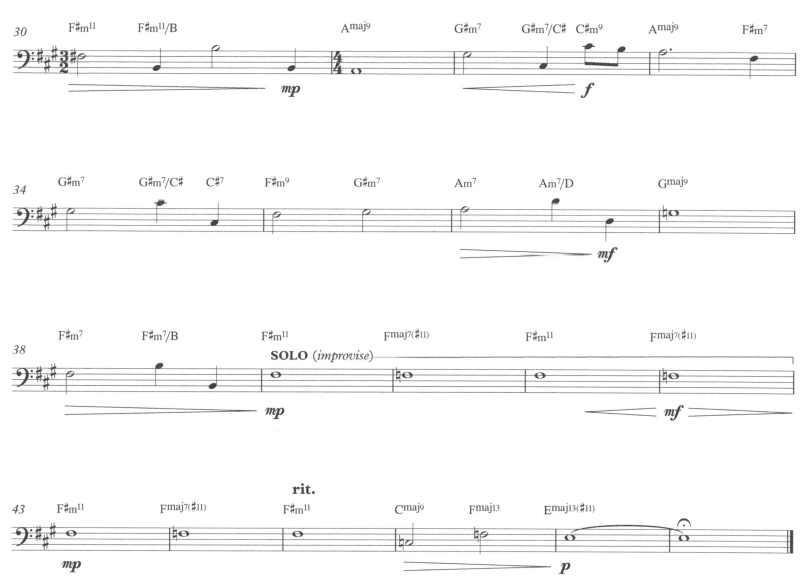

3. *Learned Poets*

Orlando Gibbons (1583–1625)

BOB CHILCOTT

BASS and DRUMS

4. Fire, fire!

Thomas Morley (1557–1602)

BOB CHILCOTT

BC261   **Little Jazz Madrigals**   CHILCOTT

ISBN 978-0-19-356156-4

9 780193 561564

Little Jazz Madrigals

Bob Chilcott

for SATB, piano, and optional bass and drum kit

Bass and Drum Kit part

The bass and drum parts may be played as written or used as a guide from which the player may improvise freely.

This part was prepared by Alexander Hawkins.

Duration: *c.*10 minutes

BASS and DRUMS

This work is dedicated to the LandesJugendChor (Rheinland-Palatinate),
which is sponsored by the Landesmusikrat and
funded by the Ministry for Science, Further Education and Culture

Little Jazz Madrigals

1. Sing we and chant it

Thomas Morley (1557–1602)

BOB CHILCOTT